ANIMAL TRACKERS

IN FIELDS & MEADOWS

Tessa Paul

 CRABTREE
Publishing Company

CRABTREE
Publishing Company
www.crabtreebooks.com

PMB 16A, 350 Fifth Avenue	612 Welland Avenue	73 Lime Walk
Suite 3308	St. Catharines	Headington, Oxford
New York, NY 10118	Ontario L2M 5V6	England OX3 7AD

Editor **Bobbie Kalman**
Assistant Editor **Virginia Mainprize**
Designers **Emma Humphreys-Davies Richard Shiner Melissa Stokes**

Illustrations by

Front cover: Terence Lambert; Introduction: Barry Croucher, Chris Rose, Valérie Stetton, Rod Sutterby; Richard Benson (p.26 – 27),
Robin Carter/WLAA (p.9), Fiona Currie (p.26), Barry Croucher/WLAA (p.30 – 31), Wayne Ford (p.21), Ruth Grewcock (p.9, 30),
Terence Lambert (p.10 – 11, 20 – 21), John Morris/WLAA (p.16 – 17, 28 – 29), Chris Rose (p.14, 15, 24), Chris Shields/WLAA
(p.22 – 23), Valérie Stetton (p.12 – 13), Mark Stewart/WLAA (p.8, 22), Kim Thompson (p.6 – 7), Simon Turvey/WLAA (p.18 – 19),
Mike Woods (p.14 – 15, 25); all track marks by Andrew Beckett

First printed 1997
Copyright © 1997 Marshall Cavendish Ltd.
Reprinted 2001

Cataloging-in-Publication Data

Paul, Tessa
In fields and meadows / Tessa Paul
p. cm. – – (Animal Trackers)
Includes index.
Summary: A guide to finding animals that live in open, grassy spaces by identifying their tracks, their nests, the sounds they make,
and other marks they make to show they have been in the area.
ISBN 0-86505-585-8 (RLB) – – ISBN 0-86505-593-9 (paper)
1. Meadow animals – Juvenile literature.
2. Animal tracks – Juvenile literature. [1. Meadow animals. 2. Animal tracks.]
I. Title.   II. Series: Paul, Tessa . Animal trackers .
QL115.5.P38   1997   599.1746 – –dc21   96-39671   CIP LC

Printed and bound in Malaysia

CONTENTS

INTRODUCTION

A field or a meadow may look wide and empty. All you can see is grass, with a clump of trees here and there.

But the grass is home to many animals, big and small. Most of them are shy and hide from people. Many come out only at night. Some have fur the same color as the shadows on the grass. When these animals stand still, they are very hard to see. Some creatures live in holes in the ground. Others build homes in the grass. Birds hide their nests in secret places.

If you look carefully, you can find signs that help you track these animals. All of them leave their marks. They scatter food. They chew on plants. They shed their fur and feathers.

This book will help you find many animals that live in grassy spaces. Beautiful color pictures show you how these animals look. You will learn about their nests and dens. You will discover where they live and how they build their homes. Soon, you will become a real animal tracker!

DEER MOUSE

Deer mice live in fields, forests, towns, and cities. You will even find them in the desert and the far north. They sleep during the day and come out at night. They like to eat seeds, berries, nuts, and insects.

HOUSE MOVES
Nests are balls of grass, lined with fluff. They are hidden in the grass or under a log. When the nest gets dirty, mice build a new one.

DAINTY BITES
Mice leave small, neat tooth marks on mushrooms and fruit. You may see these tiny feeding signs.

PIT-PAT
Deer mice have tiny feet. You must look very carefully to find their tracks.

SHARED HOMES
Where winters are cold, deer mice huddle together for warmth. If disturbed, they squeak loudly.

LITTLE DRUMMERS
When deer mice are frightened, they drum the ground with their front paws.

AT THE DOOR

Deer mice are clean and like to groom themselves. If you look very carefully, you may see bits of hair and fur at their nest entrances.

PRAIRIE DOG

Thousands of prairie dogs live together underground in dog towns. Like watch dogs, they guard the entrance to their homes. If there is danger, they bark like dogs. But these animals are not dogs – they are a type of ground squirrel.

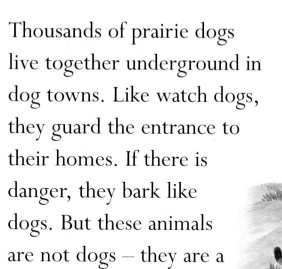

NEAT 'N CLEAN
Prairie dogs dig side tunnels. Some of these tunnels are used as toilet rooms.

DOG TOWNS

Prairie dog families are called coteries. Each has its own living space, but they share tunnels with other families. The rooms and tunnels stretch for miles.

HILLS OF HOME

Mounds of earth at each entrance keep water out of the den. Prairie dogs use the mounds as look-out posts.

9

Prairie dogs have busy days. When the sun rises, they get up and crawl out of their tunnels. For the next two hours, they search for plants and grasses which they either eat themselves or feed to their young.

Then, dogs from the same family clean each other. They take dust baths, play, and lie in the sun. At noon, they go back underground for a nap. In the afternoon, they eat again until the sun sets.

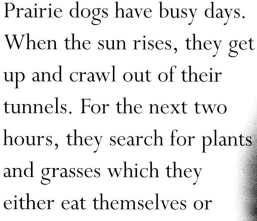

LITTLE PESTS
They love farm crops. They dig up roots and eat corn. To protect their fields, some farmers hunt prairie dogs.

GUARD MARKS
When they keep guard, prairie dogs stand on their back legs. Their feet leave a firm print.

SHELLING NUTS
They use their strong front teeth to split open nuts. Look for broken nut shells.

IN THE NURSERY

The mother builds a nest of grass and has her babies. Other dogs, even from her own coterie, must keep away. In five weeks, the babies leave the nest, and the coterie comes together again.

BARN OWL

Barn owls hunt at night. Their eyes are twice as good as ours are in the day. Their hearing is even better. A barn owl can turn its head round and hear a little mouse running on the ground. The owl swoops down and catches the mouse in its sharp claws. Barn owls are so fast and quiet that all you may hear is a gentle rustle on the ground.

OWL CALLS
Listen carefully for owl noises at night. They scream and hiss. They also grunt and snap their beaks.

SILENT FLIGHT
Because they have soft, fluffy feathers, barn owls make no noise when they fly. They hold their wings wide and glide.

HARD NESTS
Barn owls do not build a nest. They lay their eggs on bare wood in hollow trees or on barn floors. They even lay them on the cold stone of caves and buildings. Mother owls lay between five and eight eggs but not all at the same time. The first egg laid is the first to hatch.

SIGNS OF EATING
On the ground, under trees, you may find owl pellets. These are balls of bone, fur, and feather. Owls spit these out after they have eaten.

OPEN SPACES
Barn owls live on the forest edge or in open country. In towns, they hunt in empty lots, parks, and cemeteries.

POWER HOOKS
Owls have long, hooked claws called talons. Their feet are covered with short hair.

13

MOLE

Moles spend most of their lives underground. They have tiny, weak eyes, and some are blind. They feel their way through the dark earth with the stiff hairs around their mouth and nose. The mole is suited to life in the earth. It has short legs, a streamlined body, and a pointed nose.

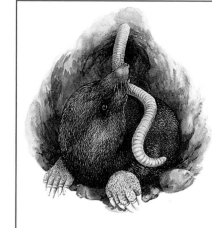

EASY DINING
Moles are big eaters. They eat one-and-a-half times their body weight each day. Moles do not hunt for food. They find the worms and grubs that crawl into their tunnels.

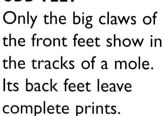

ODD FEET
Only the big claws of the front feet show in the tracks of a mole. Its back feet leave complete prints.

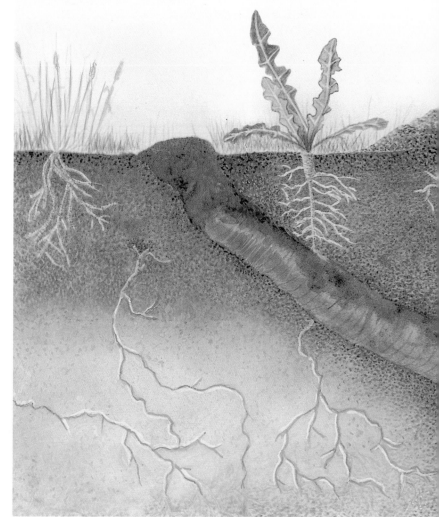

MOLE HILLS

When digging tunnels, moles use their nails and front paws to loosen the earth. Then they turn around and push the earth to the top. Piles of earth show the tunnel entrances.

DIFFERENT TUNNELS

Moles search for food in shallow tunnels. They dig deeper tunnels for their homes and nests.

THRUSH

The thrush has a lovely song. If you listen, you will hear little tunes with different musical notes. Thrushes usually live in woods. Sometimes, you will spot them in bushes and low trees in gardens. They eat berries, insects, worms, and slugs. Often, you can see these birds hopping on the ground, looking for food.

PRETTY EGGS

The thrush makes a tidy nest. First, it weaves a little basket of moss, leaves, and small roots. Inside the basket, it makes a smooth bowl of hard mud. It lays four eggs in spring. The eggshells are blue with brown spots. The father helps the mother feed the baby birds.

TAKE OFF

Some birds take a little run on the ground before they start to fly. Thrushes just jump straight up into the air.

LOW HOPS
These birds do not fly very high. They leap up from the ground and fly fast into the bushes. Sometimes, they swoop and curve through the air.

SPOTTED SIGNS
Soft dots mark the underpart of the bird. It has pointed wings, and the tail is long for such a small bird.

SECRET PLACES
You may find a little nest on the branch of a bush or hidden in the leaves of a hedge. Never touch a nest if there are eggs or babies inside.

FOX

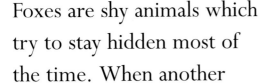

Foxes are shy animals which try to stay hidden most of the time. When another animal moves out of its den, foxes take over. They often have more than one den. If there is any danger, they move to a safer den.

SMALL AND TASTY

Foxes eat small animals, such as rats, voles, and mice. They also enjoy earthworms and insects. When foxes eat birds, they leave a pile of broken feathers and crushed bones.

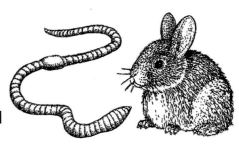

NEAT EATS

Foxes love eggs and sometimes raid farmers' chicken coops. You can tell when a fox has eaten an egg. One end will be cleanly and neatly bitten off.

CLOSE TO HOME

A mother nurses her cubs. Parents take turns hunting food for the cubs, which are kept safely near the den.

FINDING FOXES

Foxes give a short, sharp bark. They call to warn each other of danger. They also leave a musty smell behind them. You can smell it near the dens or where they have been eating.

USEFUL TAILS

The bushy tail helps the fox to keep its balance when pouncing after food. Look for tufts of foxes' fur left on fences or garden gates.

DOG-LIKE

Foxes' tracks look like those of a dog. Foxes walking in snow leave a straight line of tracks.

PRONGHORN

Pronghorns are gentle, curious, and fun-loving antelope. They may run beside cars for the fun of the race. With their excellent eyesight they can see for miles. If you spot one, keep very still. It will only run if it sees sudden movement.

LAND MARKS
The pronghorn is the fastest running animal living in North America. Its tracks may be blurred.

GENTLE FIGHTS
When males quarrel over a female, they lower their heads and stare at each other. Finally one will leave. They seldom fight with their sharp horns.

HOME ON THE RANGE
Pronghorns are animals of the grass-lands and prairies. They live in wide, open spaces.

TRAVELING GROUPS
These animals live together in small herds, but families often graze together away from the group.

UNDER THE SNOW
In winter, pronghorns scrape the ground looking for food. You can see these scratch marks in the snow.

TELL-TALE SIGHT
Pronghorns are well camouflaged. It is difficult to see them against the prairie grass. However, you can see their white rumps flashing in the sun when they run.

COYOTE

Coyotes are found in most of North America. They live in forests and on the prairies, in hot and cold climates. Some have moved near farms and towns. They raid chicken coops, hunt mice and rats, and eat garbage.

FURRY FEET
You may see fuzzy fur marks between the imprint of their pads.

FAMILY SING-ALONG
At night, you may hear coyotes howling. One starts with a sad wail, and the others follow. The pups copy their parents. Hunting coyotes howl to tell other coyotes to keep away.

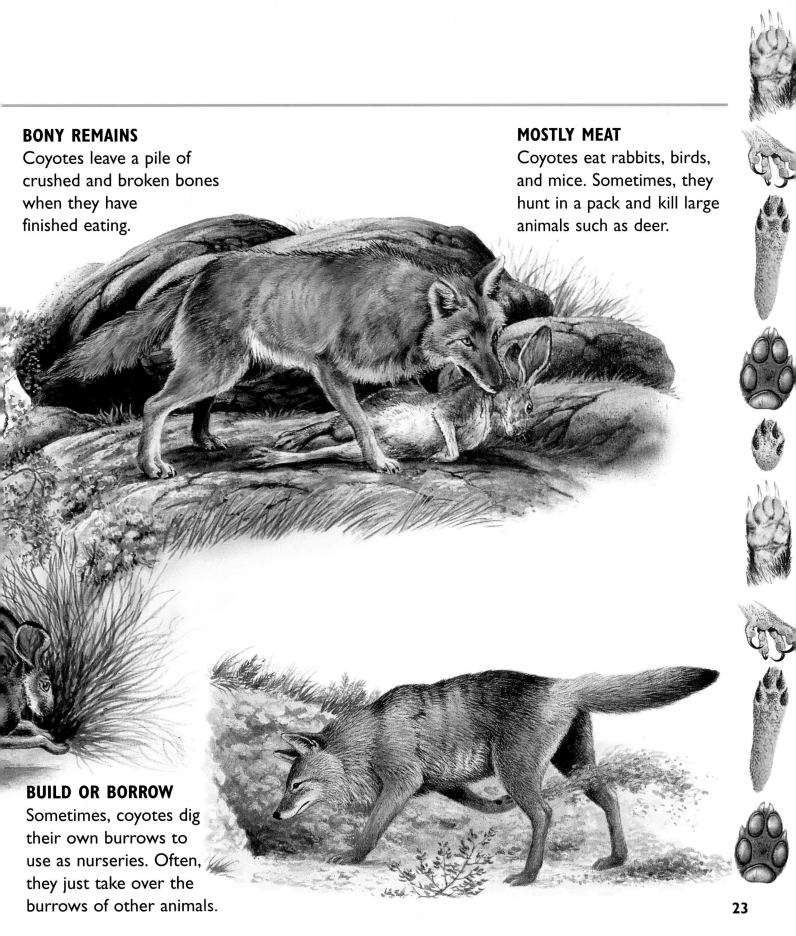

BONY REMAINS
Coyotes leave a pile of crushed and broken bones when they have finished eating.

MOSTLY MEAT
Coyotes eat rabbits, birds, and mice. Sometimes, they hunt in a pack and kill large animals such as deer.

BUILD OR BORROW
Sometimes, coyotes dig their own burrows to use as nurseries. Often, they just take over the burrows of other animals.

RABBIT

Rabbits are found all over the world. They hide in the grass during the day. At dusk, you may see them in little groups, nibbling grass, twigs, and buds.

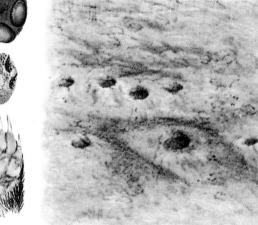

SAFE HOMES
Mother rabbits build nests in small hollows. They line them with grass and their own fur. They have five or six babies three or four times a year.

BACK TO FRONT
When rabbits hop, they push their back legs over their front paws.

HIDING PLACES

Rabbits live in shallow holes called forms. Outside these, you may see a pile of hard rabbit droppings called pellets.

VEGETABLE DIET

These animals eat grass and wild flowers. They also dig up roots and bulbs and love carrots. Farmers and gardeners think rabbits are pests.

DEER

Deer are shy animals that live in open places near the edge of the forest. They hide during most of the day. At dusk and dawn, they come out to eat. In the spring and summer, they feed on tender, young grasses and leaves. In the winter, they chew small branches and strip the bark off trees.

SHEDDING
The male deer, the bucks, have antlers. They use them to fight other bucks when looking for a mate. Each year, they shed their antlers and grow new ones. You may find an old antler on the ground.

MUD BATHS
During the mating season, some deer roll in muddy pools. You may see hair and fur left in the mud.

SHARP MARKS
Deer leave long, pointed prints.

PRIVATE TIME
The doe hides under a bush to have her babies.

PIKA

LIGHT TRACKS
The tracks are small and difficult to see.

Pikas are shy, furry animals, the size of a hamster. They live in rocky places and sit on ledges watching the world below. Because their gray fur matches the rocks, pikas are difficult to see. They make a high-pitched "peek" sound to tell other animals to keep away and warn of danger. When its most dangerous enemy, the weasel, is near, the pika becomes very quiet and makes no sound at all.

HARVEST TIME
All summer, pikas collect grass and other plants and dry them in the sun. In one day, a pika makes over 100 trips building its haystack.

ROCK RABBITS

Pikas are in the same family as rabbits, but they have short, round ears. Unlike rabbits, their back and front legs are the same length.

CAVE HOMES

Mothers build nests of dried grass under rocks. They have three or four babies each summer.

HARE

During the day, hares rest in shallow holes called forms. They come out at night to eat. They follow well-used trails to their feeding areas. You can see these runways cut through the grass or in the snow.

LUCKY LEGS
When frightened, hares run away and hide. They have long, strong back legs and can run very fast.

GNAW AND SLICE
In summer, hares eat plant shoots. Look for a clean, slanted cut. In winter, they eat bark. You can see where they have stripped it off at the bottom of a tree or bush.

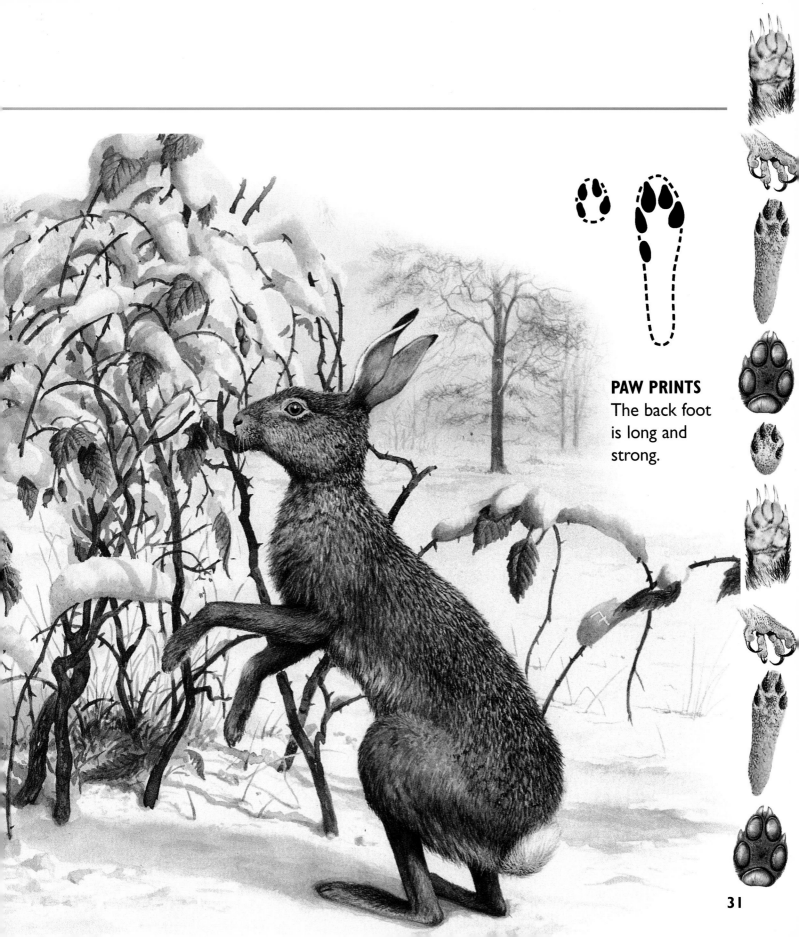

PAW PRINTS
The back foot is long and strong.

INDEX

GLOSSARY

Burrow - The tunnel or hole in the ground dug by an animal for its home.

Buck - A male deer is called a buck, so is a male rabbit.

Camouflage - Many animals blend with the color of the place where they live. This is called camouflage. Camouflage protects an animal from its enemies and hides it when it is trying to catch other animals.

Colony - A large group of animals of the same kind living together is called a colony. They build their nests or dens in one shared place.

Coterie - A family of prairie dogs is called a coterie.

Den - The home or hiding place of a wild animal.

Doe - A female deer is called a doe, so is a female rabbit.

Form- A shallow hole in the earth or grass. Some animals use forms as their home or resting place.

Pellets - Small, hard balls of animal droppings. Owl pellets are balls of fur and bone that an owl spits up after it has eaten.